Just Wish
I Had Known

A Guide to Opening a Dental Practice

Joy N. McDaniel, DMD

WestBow
PRESS®
A DIVISION OF THOMAS NELSON
& ZONDERVAN

Scriptures taken from the Holy Bible, New International Version®, NIV®. Copyright © 1973, 1978, 1984, 2011 by Biblica, Inc.™ Used by permission of Zondervan. All rights reserved worldwide. www.zondervan.com The "NIV" and "New International Version" are trademarks registered in the United States Patent and Trademark Office by Biblica, Inc.™

WestBow Press books may be ordered through booksellers or by contacting:

WestBow Press
A Division of Thomas Nelson & Zondervan
1663 Liberty Drive
Bloomington, IN 47403
www.westbowpress.com
1 (866) 928-1240

ISBN: 978-1-9736-4669-3 (sc)
ISBN: 978-1-9736-4670-9 (e)

Library of Congress Control Number: 2018913985

Print information available on the last page.

WestBow Press rev. date: 4/24/2019

Contents

Acknowledgments

Thank you to my very best friend, my husband, Sedrick. I'm blessed beyond measure to have such a wonderfully supportive and encouraging man in my corner. You signed up to marry a dentist having no clue what that meant. Thank you for sharing your life with me. I'm loving every minute of it.

Thanks to all of my parents for allowing me to grow strong. Each of you has left your unique fingerprint on my life. I have two sets of loving parents and several honorary parents across the country who have invested in my future as if it were their own. A special thanks to my in-laws who welcomed me into the family with open arms from the very first day we met. I wear the McDaniel name with pride.

The kiddos are the laughter I never knew I needed, until I truly needed it. Thank you Tristan, Sarah, and Madison, for bringing a forever smile to the McDaniel household, no matter how near or far you may be.

Thanks to my closest friends; friends who knew me long before my dentistry journey. You all continue to hold my ladder steady and encourage me to climb higher, even when I don't know if I can take another step. This is a true sign of how strong our bond will forever be.

Thanks to my spiritual parents and pastors who taught me, with their actions, that there is true power in sowing and reaping. There is unspeakable power in keeping my faith in God, no matter how tough the storm may be.

I will forever be grateful for all those who asked me, "How did you do it?" because it allowed me the opportunity to say, "Just wish I had known."

Instead of being discouraged by opposition, be
encouraged by it, knowing that on the other side of
that difficulty is a new level of your destiny.
—Unknown

Who Am I?

I was born and raised in the beautiful state of North Carolina, where I spent the first half of my life. We lived in a small town about twenty minutes outside of Greensboro, North Carolina, which is such a beautiful part of the country. After graduating from high school, I attended Florida A&M University in Tallahassee. I graduated with my bachelor's degree in psychology with a minor in pre-dentistry and then returned to North Carolina. For the next year and a half, I worked with my mother at a large nonprofit organization that manages childcare resources across the state. While working there, I applied to dental school and rested my brain from undergraduate school and the relentless Florida sunshine.

During my time between undergrad and dental school, I was offered an amazing opportunity to attend the very first dental post-baccalaureate program in the country at UCSF School of Dentistry in San Francisco. This pre-dentistry program is an excellent opportunity for those who are underrepresented in this field and desire to pursue a career in dentistry. The UCSF Post-Baccalaureate program opens doors that enables minorities to competitively apply to dental school. The great Dr. Harvey Brody, along with Dr. Charles Alexander, were the program founders and directors at the time I attended in 1999. I was in the second class of the program's existence, and now in 2018, it is still running strong and has set the example for many similar programs to begin across the country.

Dr. Brody was (and still is) such a wonderful blessing to me and so many others. His heart and compassion for all people and knowledge of the field of dentistry is enormous. He has worked in the field of dentistry for over sixty years across America from Washington DC to San Francisco. Having the opportunity to sit under him and now beside him as a colleague is an honor beyond words. I am so grateful for Dr. Brody and the sacrifices he made in order to ensure that those underrepresented can have a fighting chance to pursue a career in this competitive and rewarding field of medicine.

According to the American Dental Association's 2011 publication *Something to Smile About: Careers in Dentistry*, African Americans, Hispanics, and Native Americans made up only 12 percent of the students attending dental school, even though they made up 30 percent of the general population, and that percentage is expected to increase to 50 percent by 2050 (Dental Association n.d.). This report also notes that minority patients are more likely to establish a routine plan of care with a dentist they can better relate to and who shares their language and culture. After successfully completing the UCSF Post-Baccalaureate program, I was accepted at both Meharry Medical College-School of Dentistry in Nashville and Temple University School of Dentistry in Philadelphia.

I chose to attend Temple University, mainly because of the "snow." Anyone who graduated from Temple School of Dentistry before 2004 will surely recall that this word was used by a dental school recruiter during our interview and tour. He respectfully referred to the massive numbers of patients who would pour into the dental school daily to receive treatment by the students as "snow." I recall him saying Philadelphia has a lot of snow in the wintertime outside, and Temple Dental has a lot of snow year-round inside the school. Temple Dental remains proud of their significant patient population, because students have never had a problem finding patients to work on. As a matter of fact, we would unfortunately have to turn patients away on some of the busier days in the clinics.

I knew I wanted to spend my time as a clinician rather than do research after graduation, so having numerous patients to work on and learn from was very important to me during my dental school education. Dental school itself was not easy, but attending dental school was, in hindsight, one of the best choices I ever made. I am so grateful for the education, dental training, and life experiences I received at Temple Dental.

After graduating, receiving my Doctor of Dental Medicine (DMD) degree and Pennsylvania dental license, I applied for a job working for a contract company who supplied civilian dental employees nationwide for the US Army. My first assignment was at Fort Bragg in North Carolina. I can clearly recall shedding a few tears when I heard my first assignment was at Fort Bragg; this was the very last place on earth I wanted to go. Growing up in North Carolina, I remembered traveling through Fort Bragg's military base on the way to see my grandmother in Lumberton. When I was a child, there was nothing in Fort Bragg but red clay, Humvees, and soldiers. Preparing to leave the big, bustling city of Philadelphia to return to the small dusty town of Fayetteville did not appeal to me at all. Little did I know that God had amazing plans for me in all of that red clay and dust.

The first great surprise was that Fayetteville had grown tremendously since my childhood, and it wasn't a bad place to live. Yes, there was still red clay, Humvees, and soldiers, but the population had expanded so much beyond the US Army base, and I was pleasantly surprised. This was where I grew in my dental career and ultimately opened my own dental practice. This was also where my spiritual foundation grew more than I could have expected. Best of all, this was where I met and married Sedrick, my very best friend.

Needless to say, my nine-plus years living in Fayetteville were no mistake, after all. I am grateful that we often don't get what we ask for, but we get what we need. Even though I didn't understand the plans God had for me, letting go of the reins of my life and giving them to Him made a world of difference in this path I called my life. I am very grateful to God for ordering and directing my steps. This journey brought the Bible scripture Jeremiah 29:11 to life: "'For I know the plans I have for you,' declares the Lord, 'plans to prosper you and not to harm you, plans to give you hope and a future'" (NIV).

Writing this book is another one of those ordered steps, and as of this very moment, why I've been asked to do this still remains a mystery to me. However, I have learned over the years that it's best to trust God and to rest in the palm of His hand as He orders our paths in life, no matter where they may lead us, even to the red clay and dust.

Introduction

In their hearts humans plan their course, but the
LORD establishes their steps. (Proverbs 16:9 NIV)

I'm writing this book with senior dental students and dentists
just aching to open their own dental practice in mind. This
book is in no way a knock against what we were taught in dental
school. I'm sure whatever dental school you attended taught you,
just as mine did, how to be the best clinician possible. However,
they only had four years to make that happen, so there are many
valuable lessons a formal dental school education cannot cover.
There are several topics that were not taught that I wish I had
known before stepping out and embarking on the ownership
of Oasis Dental, my first dental practice. The intention of this
book is not to question your intelligence. It is a brief guide to
help you make wiser decisions or to cause to you pause for a
moment before opening your own practice, which could be a
life-changing decision.

Throughout the process of establishing and operating my
dental practice, there were many things people chose not to tell
me, forgot to explain, or just plain didn't want me to know. I am
of the complete opposite mindset. I have no problem screaming

to the top of the rafters, "Hey, look at what I did; please do the opposite." I can even say, "Repeat after me, because this worked." I do not claim to know everything about starting a dental practice, but what I learned through experience alone, I wish someone had told me. It's just that plain and simple.

Would I have listened? Maybe. If many of us can be transparent, we would say that after dental school, we thought we knew everything. Our brains had been conditioned to hold so many facts that no one could convince us that we were not the smartest people on the face of the earth. Wisdom says otherwise, and I agree with wisdom. Having the information in this book before I started my business would have saved me from many headaches, sleepless nights, and tears of frustration. I feel there is something in this book that will give you reason to say, "Oh, yeah, that's a great idea. I'm so glad she told me that." There are plenty of books on why you should own your own small business, but this book is different. It's an open and transparent guide about all the things I wish I had known before and during the process of opening my dental practice.

CHAPTER 1

In Business? Who, Me?

Preparation is never lost time.

-Bishop E.B. Herman, Harvest Family
Church, Fayetteville, North Carolina

Being a competent clinician does not make you a competent business owner or leader. Yes, you say that you know this, but do you really? I didn't. I was taught how to do beautiful crowns and bridges, place implants, and fabricate dentures, and I can extract teeth with the best of them. I have packed what feels like a million amalgams and composites. Yet I had no clue about the right way to manage and run a business.

A few years after I opened my practice, Dr. Rosa Herman, a very wise woman, told me, "You *never* manage your business like an employee." The truth is, that summed up most of my poor management practices in one sentence. The funny thing is that Dr. Herman said this while sitting in my dental chair as a patient. She was sharing what she had learned in her own personal experience of owning a successful business for many years.

For almost seven years, I worked for other dentists as an associate, and after I opened my own practice, I made the conscience decision to manage my business like I thought I wanted my previous employers to manage their practices. I thought this would make me the best boss in the world. Don't expect praise if you adopt this type of management style because it is not coming. I was always taught to live by the biblical verse, "So in everything, do to others what you would have them do to you" (Matthew 7:12 NIV). This is a very true statement. However, as it applies to a business, "Don't run over your employees, but still run your business" would be a good translation.

I managed my employees as if they were my best friends. I have always been known to have a very soft heart and a giving personality. When walking down some of the roughest, inner-city streets of Philadelphia surrounding our campus, I was typically the one reaching in my pocket to give cash to the guy laying on a piece of cardboard in the middle of the sidewalk. Many of my classmates would step past him as if he were not even there. No, they were not mean or heartless people; they were better described as street smart. What my classmates understood that I did not was that it would only take one criminally-minded person to watch me shuffle around inside my purse for cash and attack me, taking everything I had. Thank God I never got attacked on the streets of Philadelphia. Unfortunately, I was "attacked" in various ways in the safety of my own dental practice. I would often hear a sob story about how someone was struggling financially, and I would literally give away my dental services. Most often, my method of giving would be by not charging the full price for a service.

I recall my office manager saying, "Doc, you cannot keep doing this." At one point, I recall her reviewing the financials and stating, "I'm going to limit you to doing this for only one patient per quarter." In hindsight, the funniest part was that she was as soft as I was, so the limit she set never really stuck.

We will discuss later on why hiring an office manager with a heart of gold and a marshmallow interior was a poor choice on my part. Don't think I didn't care for her; she was a wonderful person and would have fit best as the billing/insurance specialist in the office, which is what she did exceptionally well. As the manager of the office, not so much. Whoever is managing the practice needs to be a bulldog of sorts. Respectful and kind, but a bulldog nonetheless. Most of the patients who benefited from the discounted and free services had no clue they had gotten one over on me. We almost never told anyone. I am no longer crying over the milk I spilt, but I am reminded of how running a practice with that mindset does not pay the bills, the staff, or myself.

Another example of how I managed my office like an employee: the office covered the expenses of a dental conference trip to Las Vegas for the entire dental team. The team's flights, hotel, and conference fees were paid in full by the practice. What dentist would not want to do that for their entire team? While in Las Vegas, I also treated everyone to the Cirque du Soleil performance of "O." Honestly, how can anyone travel to Las Vegas and not see one of the Cirque performances? I failed to mention this was in our first year. Six months after the trip, I was wondering why in the world I approved it. At the time of arranging the trip, I had all good intentions. I only knew that there was cash in the bank to cover the conference expenses, but I did not consider the unexpected expenses we might face after we returned. Though we gained valuable knowledge to help our practice thrive, and the team building was wonderful, I failed to consider that the office would be closed and not producing anything during this trip.

Another key management mistake I made during this phase was when I decided to start all of my dental team off at the top range of their salaries, including full benefits. The benefits included paid vacation and paid federal holidays off, along with health care coverage. None of these things, in and of themselves, are bad to offer your team; just consider what phase of the practice to offer them in. Year one may not be the best time to do this.

Deciding to start a new practice and stock some of the highest quality dental equipment on the market was another decision I would reconsider. With this next comment, don't think I am anti-dental supply companies. They serve an important purpose. However, these firms are in the business of selling dental supplies: chairs, equipment, delivery systems, management software systems, and so on. I now realize good-quality, discounted equipment exists on the discounted equipment websites for a reason. Why didn't I think of that? I often find myself shopping for quality personal items at a discounted price. I still have no clue why I didn't consider that same shopping method for my practice. What patient really cares if your autoclave sterilizer is platinum plated and the dental chair has hand-stitched Italian leather? Okay, mine were not either, but with the price I paid for those new items, they should have been.

The dental supply company I purchased most of my supplies from flew me, all expenses paid, to one of the top dental equipment factories to see how their products were made. The firm wined and dined me and about twenty other dentists for the weekend. Needless to say, I took the bait; their sales tactic worked wonders. I'm not saying that the dental equipment I purchased wasn't worth the purchase price. I never needed to replace those delivery units or chairs. However, as a new practice, this Mercedes-Benz version of the dental chair and delivery system was well beyond our operating budget, and I was unfortunately blinded by the bling. There was an atmosphere and a standard that I desired for my personal office that I didn't find in the offices where I previously worked. I desired an oasis, hence the name of my practice was born, Oasis Dental.

The name of my practice was not just a catchy phrase; it was truly what I desired my patients to experience every time they entered our doors. From the feedback we received, they did, but at what cost to the overall profit of the practice? I now understand that I could have provided a similar atmosphere on a much more practical budget, which would have allowed me to have the oasis in my mind that I was striving to provide for my dental team and patients.

Managing your practice like an employee will stress you out. That management style becomes more about pleasing those around you versus focusing on the bottom line of what needs to be done. I'm not saying to never take your dental team on an all-expense-paid conference or to pay them minimum wage. I'm not saying your equipment needs to be rusted out and uncomfortable for your patients. I am, however, suggesting that you pace yourself. All of those things can and will come, with earned time. None of it has to be acquired in full on opening day.

The more I talk to dentists, the more I realize I wasn't the only one who made these mistakes. Dentistry is enjoyable, rewarding, and fun, yet owning your own practice can be scary, traumatizing, dramatic, and a headache: anything but fun. So what was the lesson in all of the things I endured as a first-time business owner? As a faithful Christian, I felt compelled to ask God, "What was the purpose of all of this? Why did you allow me, of all people, to experience this?"

I honestly felt like God clearly said, "It was not just about you."

Every time I had a "Why me?" moment, I would encounter colleagues who'd ask my advice on various aspects of how I operated my dental practice, and I was amazed at how our stories were similar. Interestingly, many of the lessons I'd already learned, they had not discovered yet after many years in business. Having my own practice was not a mistake. I understand that there were colleagues I needed to meet and patients I needed to treat; I wanted to give them a positive dental experience and aid them in conquering their fear of the dentist. Many of the team members who I hired were looking for a different place to work because their previous dental jobs were not as ideal as they wanted them to be. These are some of the ways it was confirmed that owning my practice was not just all about me. What a humbling and selfless experience and revelation.

So now what? Now I have an opportunity to share some of what I did right and wrong in the hopes that this information will help others. The dental community can seem small at times, and yet we are not always available to share our knowledge with each other. If you ask for assistance, many colleagues may seem reluctant because helping you succeed may take patients away from their practice. Fortunately, there are some who will aid you without the fear of creating competition in their neighborhoods. Those of us willing to help would rather see others learn from the lessons we've learned so they won't have to endure the heartaches, frustrations, and disappointments when you first open your own practice.

Do I claim to have all the answers? Absolutely not. But I really just wish I had known these things before I decided to open my own dental practice. Not to belabor the point, but I feel the need to repeat that this book's intent is not to discourage anyone from opening their own dental practice. It has been designed to help open your eyes to what you may have never thought of in the process of becoming a dental practice owner.

There are a few "must dos" I think you should consider before you start:

1. Hire a Certified Public Accountant (CPA). And not just any

old CPA, either. Hire someone who is an active participant in the Academy of Dental CPAs (ADCPA). No, I am not receiving any royalties from this organization, but I do recognize the benefits they offer to dentists across America. You can do an engine search online and locate a firm close to your location. I cannot think of any reasons against using a dental CPA. They have access to information that will help your practice, and they know about finances for dental practitioners that general CPAs may not be aware of. I appreciate the fact that the CPAs who belong to the ADCPA are a tight-knit community, working across state lines. If your firm is ever faced with a challenge with regards to your practice, or when new laws and policies are passed, they are able to swiftly pass the information on to their network of colleagues to share the information they are privy to. It truly is a wonderful organization that has figured out how to benefit the dental community with their trade.

When I initially became an independent contractor, prior to opening my dental practice, the first CPA I hired was not an ADCPA member, and I paid dearly (literally) for that mistake. My first CPA had actually retired from the IRS and was very knowledgeable with standard small businesses, like hair salons and small restaurants. However, they knew nothing about the significant business differences that dentists encounter with equipment depreciation, the good will of the practice, and other topics that pertain to dental practices.

2. Hire a payroll company to do your office payroll. This is something I was told to do from day one of opening my practice, and I am so thankful for following that advice. I never had to be concerned about payroll taxes, which can be the financial demise of small businesses or, even worse, land the owner in prison if they are not paid properly. A payroll company typically charges a very small fee each time they issue checks or direct deposits.

The check stubs for my team were automatically mailed to the office on a biweekly basis, along with an itemized statement of the payroll company's fees, employee salaries, FICA, Medicare, taxes, and so on. Anything and everything I needed regarding payroll was in one nice and neat binder. Even if you have team members who pay child support or have part of their wages garnished to the IRS, the payroll company is able to handle those payments, typically at no extra charge to you.

Hiring both the dental CPA and payroll company was well worth the minimal cost. It reduced the stress of handling such important parts of the practice, allowing me to focus more on providing quality dentistry.

CHAPTER 2
Your Dental Team

People are waiting on the other side of your obedience.

– Pastor Dave Minton, Capital Christian Center, Lacey, Washington

One of the best decisions I ever made in practice was choosing my team: selecting people I actually liked as individuals. Maybe that seems strange, but there are many people who hire staff based on experience and quality of work *only*. Yes, those traits are key to the success of your business. However, if you find yourself exhaling and rolling your eyes when you think about a particular team member or pausing for deep prayer while asking God for inner peace before entering the building, dreading the possibility that a certain team member's negative attitude has permeated throughout the office, this makes for a very long, uncomfortable workday. When the attitude of an employee negatively affects the office atmosphere whenever they're around, this is a red flag, a warning that something needs to change.

The people I chose actually enjoyed each other's company, and I would not change that decision for anything in the world. I have worked in several offices where team members could not stand the sight of each other. They were highly qualified in doing their jobs, however they did not communicate well, they refused to help each other out, and there was constant back-biting and running to the supervisors complaining about the most insignificant things. More often than not, each of them assumed the actions of the other were intentionally negative, and they refused to give each other the benefit of the doubt. There was such a negative atmosphere in the air that it didn't matter whether they performed their task well or not. There was no trust amongst them and for years they endured the negative work environment. There had been several attempts to heal their hurts with multiple team-building exercises and meetings with supervisors and even mediators, but the drama continued.

I learned a great lesson: people have to want their current situation to change before change can happen. I often wonder if they secretly enjoyed the drama; it was obvious they didn't want it to go away. Team members who truly enjoy each other's presence will work hard to do whatever it takes to help each other in the office. This is done not because they have to, but because they want to.

I encourage offering continuing education classes to your staff. Many practice owners say, "If they want classes, they need to take them outside of my time." That is such a poor attitude to have about your team's growth. Let's remember that their continuing dental education brings value to your practice. These opportunities can also enhance your team's self-worth because they are given the opportunity to grow in their field and contribute to the development of your practice.

Personally, I'm not interested in sitting in every single class offered for dental professionals, not because I don't enjoy learning new things, but some topics are either irrelevant to my particular practice or are, let's face it, boring. My team, on the other hand, enjoyed and appreciated going to classes, learning something new, and expanding their resumes. They typically got to spend four to eight hours per class doing something outside of their typical day-to-day routine. This regular training makes your team members valuable and necessary to the practice, a kind of job security. The cost is minimal when looking at the overall benefits.

Another team builder was when we attended an annual dental conference in Las Vegas. How much fun was that? Lots. I had three rules for them: show up to the classes, don't embarrass yourself or the practice, and have fun. Everyone did exactly that. For some, this was the very first time they had ever been on an airplane or gone out of the state of North Carolina. The trip to Las Vegas did more than just give them a few education credits; it actually allowed them an opportunity to see things they had never experienced before. This was very rewarding for me, as well. As rewarding as this was for my team building, I don't recommend committing to such an expense during your first year in business. We will discuss this in more detail in future chapters. Once you have established a solid continuing education budget for the practice, this type experience for your team can be truly invaluable.

Provide dental services for your dental team and their immediate family for free or at significantly discounted rates. What a great advertisement for your practice. This idea is wisdom at its best. Once I thought about it more, I realized treating my team members' spouses and children would be brilliant for several reasons: they wouldn't have to take time off work in order to take family members to other offices, they'd have personal experience with my work to recommend my practice, and it also added to their benefits package. I scheduled their family members during times that would not interrupt regular patient care, like after hours. If they had to come in during regular office hours, the team member was able to continue working while I treated their spouse or child; some even assisted, while others chose to stay out of the operatory. It was quite funny how they could switch from dental assistant to Mommy in half a second; it was kind of hilarious watching that transition.

We offered minor orthodontic treatment for adults, and one of my patients when we started offering this service was my office manager. It was wonderful having her actively in ortho while talking to the patients about that part of their treatment plan. She was able to give a personal experience to them regarding that particular service. As a matter of fact, I had many team members and their families advertising the services we offered by word of mouth; this was the best marketing tool ever. Team members were able to confidently reassure nervous or hesitant patients that they were in good hands by telling them of their own personal experience as a patient in my chair. It was even better when the mom-to-mom discussions would take place in the waiting room, as a nervous mother was pacing the floor, waiting to see if their child was going to survive their first dental injection. Needless to say, they all did, and my team member would help reassure the parents by informing them we had completed dental treatment on their children too, and all was well.

In the rare cases when someone needed lab work, I would charge them the lab fees. For any of you who do not want to have a "non-production visit," consider coming in on a day off or have an "office dental day" just for the team and their family. Bring pizza and movies for the kids and coffee and doughnuts for the spouses while they wait to be seen. The team works as normal, unless they are the patient. This does not have to be a draining experience for you or your practice, but the overall benefit it provides is worth considering.

Incentives for your team can be another great team builder. This is an ideal way to show your team how much you appreciate their hard work and dedication. My CPA suggested that I be flexible with bonuses and not determine a set time or date for bonuses to be given. People tend to expect them when they are given on a regular schedule, like the infamous Christmas bonus people may expect and budget for. Most forget that bonuses should be earned and not a given. I would randomly provide my team with breakfast or lunch, and for the Christmas holiday, I would always be sure to give them time off and treat them to a nice lunch at a restaurant.

The bonuses were a suggestion that I followed, and it reduced the pressure to provide frequent salary increases. My suggestion is to only give bonuses when you've had a stellar month or quarter. However, cash is not the only bonus that can be given. You can give gift certificates to a spa or gift cards to dinner and a movie. For one of our office anniversaries, I surprised my team by taking them to have massages and lunch at a popular restaurant. They came to work, thinking we were doing a day of training, and instead, we loaded up in our vehicles and made a great day of gratitude. My office manager was the only one privy to the real agenda of the day. To my surprise, most of my team had never had a massage before, so needless to say, our lunch conversation after the spa treatment was quite hilarious. The ladies all enjoyed their time and knew that I appreciated all they did for the office. This was also an excellent way to build team unity, and that again is priceless.

Enable your team to succeed with the patients, even in the simple things. As an example, formulate unique methods for them to remember each patient. It can be extremely helpful to develop a way to better communicate within the office, which helps your staff feel more confident in working with patients who may only come into the office periodically. One method is to come up with cute icon that can be placed in the patient's medical record. For example, choose a rabbit to indicate the patient is fearful of the dentist or a bear to indicate the patient likes to be sedated for procedures. Consider utilizing the famous three wise monkeys (see no evil, hear no evil, speak no evil) to show that the patient doesn't want to see the dental instruments or likes it quiet throughout the procedure, so you will be sure not to be chatty. The office staff will receive so much credit for recalling something so important without the patient having to remind them every time they return. Many people fail to realize they are not your only patient, and you may have hundreds with particular desires and needs. This method is a great way to make patients feel valuable and memorable.

When your dental team feels confident and reassured that they are providing quality care, so do you.

CHAPTER 3
Marketing 101

There are several lessons to be learned from marketing mishaps. First, let's establish that there is a difference between marketing and advertising. Marketing is your brand: how you do things and how you promote your practice. Advertising is just one small aspect of marketing. An example of advertising is the billboard along the highway showing your name and a pretty smile. Marketing is much more; it includes the way you greet patients when they walk into your office and the warm moist towelette you give them to wipe their faces off before they leave the office. It is your brand. The level of marketing shows current and potential patients the quality of service you provide. Proper marketing is a way to show the pride you have in yourself, your dental team, and the practice as a whole. I often think of a popular chain Mexican restaurant that sings, "Welcome," when anyone enters their doors. Anyone who has visited this establishment will know the tune because they sing it every single time those doors open. It is a simple marketing tool that works for that restaurant.

I'm not suggesting you have a jingle or that your team become robots whenever your office door opens, but there should be some sort of routine to the things you do for your patients that sets you apart from other dental offices. Do you have a fully stocked coffee and tea bar in the waiting room? Do you have that unique xylitol gum at the check-out desk that patients cannot find in local stores? Do your team members ask about Mrs. Jones's granddaughter's dance recital she was so excited about the last time she came to the office? What do you do that makes patients not only remember but prefer you over the next office? I have a few suggestions to consider in deciding how you plan to market your practice:

1. Always have your name on everything that goes out of your office. This includes toothbrushes, pamphlets, pens, even the bag you give them their hygiene care items in. Most printers don't charge additional fees to imprint on these items, so be sure everything has your office name and phone number listed, as well as your Instagram or Facebook account. I often saw my office pens in people's hands I had never met before, and that always made me smile. Speaking of pens, don't purchase the cheapest pens you can find. No, you don't need to break the bank. However, if someone uses your pen and it falls apart in their hand or doesn't write, you indicate to them that you don't care about quality. That may not be true about the dentistry you perform, but remember, most patients have no clue what we do in their mouths. Patients will equate your marketing with the quality of other services performed.

2. Participate in health fairs or community events, where the general public can interact with you and your team. Also consider being a sponsor at a local event, program, or play. I am a firm believer in looking up the organization and seeing what they stand for before giving them your name as a sponsor. If you don't believe in what they support, be sure you politely say, "No, thank you," or "Our charity funds are already allocated for this year." Be mindful not to donate to everything that comes across

your desk. If you are even the least bit hesitant, it may be best to say no, until you have found out more information. If you let them down gently and respectfully, they'll return and inquire about your support for their next event.

3. On-screen advertising in a movie theater was one of the wisest decisions we made. Where else do you have someone's full attention as they sit in a dimly lit theatre, waiting for a movie to start? In the theater, you are almost forced to look forward, and there is nothing else to see but the screen. What a great opportunity to advertise your office information or to even do a ten-second commercial for your practice. Advertising in a movie theater actually worked well for our office and gave us more exposure to a wider audience than any other form of advertisement we used. I suggest choosing a theater that is close to your office location.

Unfortunately, we didn't do this, and in hindsight, I think that was not the best decision for us. The venue I chose was the hottest new theater in town...on the other side of the city. Hundreds of potential patients saw our ad, but they may not have wanted to drive across town to get to our office. There were several other theater options closer to the office, and if we had the financial means to advertise in all of them, I would have done that as well. If you are limited with your budget, choose a theater close to your office location. Sedrick and I are huge movie fans, so we have no problem traveling across town to the best theatre, but not everyone goes to such lengths.

I did have several of my patients tell me they saw our advertisement in the theater, and one told me he hollered out with total surprise, "That's my dentist!" Movie theaters cross all cultural, financial, and age barriers, so this gives you exposure to a very diverse population. It is well worth the investment. This type of advertisement is worth the cost. Just think about it. Very few families watch TV commercials these days. I know in our house, we use the DVR to record most of the shows we watch, and when commercials appear, we fast-forward through them. I honestly wish we had made the choice to advertise in the movie theater much earlier than we did. It would've saved us thousands of wasted dollars on failed advertisements over the years.

4. There are many social media advertising options as well, and we have all seen them as we scroll along, sometimes more of a nuisance than anything. Who really pays attention to them? Flyers come in the mail, but people rarely read them. I usually glance at the mailer, and it typically goes in the recycle bin. We did several ads in a local free magazine that was found in nice stores and restaurants in town. I liked the magazine, but it was a pricy way to advertise. I still own the copies we had ads in, and several patients informed us that they saw us in the magazine. The key to remember is, you are not advertising for the patients you already have, but for people who are not your patients yet. This was a hard reality check when we discovered those magazine ads brought us only a couple of new patients. The reality is, few people think to look on page 14 at the ad they saw in the February issue of their local magazine when they are looking for a dentist.

5. We mentioned Mrs. Jones and her granddaughter earlier. Trying to recall conversations about a patient's life can be overwhelming, so keeping small notes in their chart or in the appointment record works really well to jog your memory about their lives and preferences. If they are animal lovers, you can put an icon next to their name to indicate that, so as soon as you see them, you can bring up something regarding their pets. If your patient had a recent tragedy, it is key to make note of that as well, so you don't get caught with your foot in your mouth and ask

how Mrs. Jones's husband is doing, only to be embarrassed when she reminds you that he died three months ago.

Speaking of major life events, if your patient shares something like a birth of a child, adoption, or death of a family member, send them a card or a gift basket from the entire office; allow all of the dental team to sign the card. If a patient is getting married, offer free whitening to the bridal party. These are great ways to show you are not just concerned with their mouth but are a compassionate dentist concerned with their overall well-being and their lives. Patients will remember the little things you do outside of billing their insurance correctly and administering anesthesia well. Yes, those things are important, but as a patient, they expect you to do that anyway. Those things do not set you apart from any other good dental practice in town, but sending a nice plant to the hospital when Mrs. Jones has surgery or a restaurant gift card after giving birth to her third child is something she may never forget. Now you have a patient for life, and she'll recommend you to those closest to her.

6. Marketing also refers to the way you render treatment to your patients. How well do you administer anesthesia? Do you give the proper amount of anesthesia so that your patient is comfortable throughout the entire dental visit, but not so much that they feel numb for days? Do you consider your long-term patients valuable? Or because you've completed their treatment plan, do you pass them off as not as significant as newer patients with lots of work to be done? How do you listen to your patients? When you ask them how they are doing, do you actually pause long enough to listen to their answer, or are you asking just out of habit? Do patients feel that you care about their well-being or only the money you can profit out of their proposed treatment? How do you address mistakes made? When something is wrong with the color or fit of the crown or their insurance was billed

incorrectly, do you ignore their concerns? Do you pass them off to a third party to respond to their questions? Do you take responsibility, admit the mistakes and offer to correct them swiftly and respectfully?

Investing in advertisement alone will not take the place of implementing excellent marketing tools for your practice.

CHAPTER 4

Any Regrets?

Making the same mistake more than once is not a mistake; it's a choice.

—Unknown

Some people ask the question, "Do you have regrets about opening your practice?" My honest answer is, "No." I don't regret stepping out of my comfort zone and doing what I needed to do in order to keep my passion about dentistry going. I was slowly losing that passion daily in the offices where I had worked. I understand that making the decision to open my practice was much bigger than keeping my passion for dentistry alive. It would have been very selfish of me to think that opening a business, spending all of that time, effort, money, and even shedding tears through the process, was all about me alone. Absolutely not. God had bigger plans, and His thoughts are so much higher than ours. I know my entire staff was blessed to be employed at our office. I also know many patients received a level of care that they may not have received anywhere else had they not come to our office.

I am so glad I worked seven years as an associate in other dental practices before opening my own dental practice. Many of my classmates, before graduation, had already decided that they wanted to start their own practice directly out of dental school. There was no interest for me to do that. Am I saying that was a poor decision on their part? Absolutely not. For me, the experience I received while working for others over the years in various offices exposed me to many things I would not have experienced straight out of dental school or in a residency program. My advice is to get as much practical experience as you can prior to opening your practice. In doing this, it relieved the stress of having to figure out how to do dentistry. I could perform most dental procedures blindfolded. My main concern and focus became observing and learning how to operate a business. In hindsight, I should have invested time in a company that teaches new small business owners how to successfully manage their businesses. This is another thing we weren't taught in dental school. Your school may have included a small business class in the midst of the clinical dentistry, but probably not to the degree needed. Getting the proper advice while developing my practice would have saved me a lot of money and time, not to mention reduced my stress.

Another suggestion is to consult with a successful dentist who is in your age range or completed dental school less than ten years ago; this keeps their information more current. I had a great source who was very willing to give me her advice, however she had been in practice over twenty years. The information she candidly shared with me was wonderful, but in several cases, she could not help me because I was facing newer challenges she did not face when she opened her practice. The economy had changed drastically, along with the dental community itself. Yes, keep a wise older dentist as a resource, but when it comes to opening a new practice, someone who is closer to the stage you are currently in will be invaluable.

Don't be afraid to consult a dentist in another city or state;

they won't feel threatened by your local success. If you happen to be one of four dentists in your town, asking your neighboring colleague how they built their successful practice may not be the way to go. They may feel too competitive and that you want to poach their patients, even though we know there are typically more than enough clients in town for everyone. Finding someone who is willing to share what they did to achieve the success they have will prove to be priceless as well.

Be mindful of the economy at the time of opening your practice. An economic downturn hit when I opened mine, and this had a negative effect on most small businesses. Hit the hardest were those that offered optional services, like dentistry. As a dentist, I understand the importance of what we do, but for those who need to cut expenses in order to survive, going to the dentist twice a year for non-urgent dental care is typically on the optional list of expenses.

Discuss your desire to start a small business with a wise and practical financial advisor prior to signing for the business loan; this will benefit you in the long run. Consider someone who is savvy to the overall world economy and how it impacts us in America. This investment will be well worth your time and money, especially on the front end of starting your practice.

CHAPTER 5

When Do We Work?

An important factor to consider is exactly what you want in life. Ask yourself, do you want freedom? Do you want the ability to travel the world? Do you want to spend more time with your children and your spouse? Do you want time to volunteer at your local church or community center? What exactly do you really want out of this life? I think after answering that question, you can better decide when and how you want to work. This will help determine some of your basics, like how many hygienists will you have? How many days of the week will you work? What will your hours be? What types of patients will you serve: cash, insurance, or both? All of these things are important factors that need to be determined before opening your practice. Yes, these things can be modified, but the key is to know your reason behind the decisions that you make. It's all about your lifestyle and the lifestyle you choose for your family. Unfortunately, I did not choose in that order. I decided our hours of operation and the days of the week we would be open before determining what I wanted as a lifestyle. That made it very difficult when my lifestyle conflicted with the office hours of operation or when I wanted more time for vacations and needed to spend more time with my husband and family.

As an example, if you are the type of parent who always wants to attend all of your child's sporting events, and they play every Saturday morning, then your office shouldn't be open on Saturday mornings. If you know that you need to leave the office at least one hour prior to your weekly book club meeting in order for you to change clothes and travel across town to the meeting, then don't set your office hours to close at the time the meeting starts. These suggestions sound like common sense, but as my best friend states, "Common sense is *not* common." When you are in the midst of making a million decisions prior to opening day, you may not think these decisions through. Once the smoke clears and you settle in to your new office, discovering that you set office hours and days that conflict with the normalcy of your life can be a significant damper. Trust me, you will need that book club, mid-week Bible study, and time to watch your kid run around the track one more time in order to keep your sanity and to remember that life is good and does not revolve around dentistry. It's better to make these decisions on the front end rather than in hindsight after the sign with your office hours is posted on the front door, your website is live, and your business cards have all been printed.

I made the choice to close our office on Mondays. This was a significant benefit financially because most federal holidays happen to fall on Mondays, which many employees desire to have those days off to spend with family, and because we were already closed, we did not have to take extra time off for those holidays. My team was able to take care of most of their personal business, like doctor appointments, on Mondays. This significantly reduced the days they requested to be off. Most of my colleagues were closed on Fridays, so this decision allowed for patients who were seeking treatment on Fridays to come to our office. I actually enjoyed having my Mondays off.

When everyone else was preparing to return to work on Sunday evening, I was getting ready to enjoy one more day off. This also gave me a full workday during the week to take care of any business for the office, if needed, while other companies were open, without having to juggle time between patients to handle business matters. If we wanted to honor a particular holiday by taking extra time off, we could close on Friday and enjoy a long four-day weekend.

Schedule the office vacation days in advance. As a single practitioner, I had to do this because my team's work schedule was affected when I was gone. Most of the time, if I was out of the office, the office was closed. So out of respect for them, I would let them know as far in advance of my absence as possible. The extremely rare times I had to be gone for the day, I would try to schedule a makeup workday so their paychecks wouldn't be short.

For holiday and vacation planning, my office manager and I would sit down with a huge calendar before the end of the year and plan the vacation days in advance so the entire team would know what days we would still be open. Doing this significantly reduced the months of questions and nagging about which days we would be closed for holidays later in the year. When I got married, we left for our honeymoon the day after the wedding, and I had a dentist come in and work for that full week. That was the longest I ever trusted my practice to anyone. Granted, this dentist just so happened to be my best friend who I went to dental school with and know better than anyone. It was an easy choice. Thank you again, Dr. Jentel; this was by far the best wedding present in the world.

When arranging a substitute dentist, count your cost. In searching for a substitute dentist to work a few days for me while I was out of town on business, the common response was,

"I don't do ____." You can fill in the blank from "extractions" to "children," yet they charged top dollar per hour, and basically only did hygiene checks. Are you serious? Oh, that still makes me steam because they got paid better than me and did a quarter of the work, not to mention I still had to pay my entire team to be at work. Count your cost. It may be more cost-effective to close the office for the day. Or, you may consider establishing a coverage agreement with another local dental office who will cover your practice or emergencies while you are out. You can return the favor when they are out of their office as well.

Here are a few other questions to ask when considering hiring a locum dentist through a temp agency. Who is this dentist? Is he or she nice to patients? What is the quality of their dental work? Does he or she develop treatment plans that follow your standards? These are all things to consider before trusting your office, and reputation, to another dentist, especially in the early years when you are building your reputation in the community. My practice was young, and I was so protective of who I allowed to come into the office as a locum because they represented me. Several of my patients were new patients, and the last thing I needed was for another dentist to run them away from the practice. One more time I say, count your cost.

CHAPTER 6

Pay Yourself, You Are
an Important Bill

Before you start a business, you may hear that of all your employees, you'll be the last to get paid. My CPA was very straightforward about this fact, and it proved to be true. However, at some point, you have to pay yourself. Your personal life will continue beyond the practice, so you will still have bills to pay and other debts and things that you need to buy. Unfortunately, no one ever tells you when to start paying yourself. Once the practice was open and running, my CPA suggested that I wait about a year before adding myself to the payroll. Not many people have a year's salary saved prior to opening their dental practice. This was something I wish I had known before starting my practice. It's important to realize that you may not get paid a regular salary for quite some time. My CPA instructed me about distributions. However, only after everyone and everything else was paid—utilities, payroll, taxes, CPA, building lease, supplies, etc.—would I be able to pay myself, if there was anything left.

In the early years, what was left was not much at all. New practices are not profitable at that stage of development. You shouldn't take every dime of what remains in the bank to pay yourself, even though you may want to. The money I was able to receive through distributions was still not a consistent amount. As an associate you are used to getting paid a set salary (or at least a percentage of commission) every two weeks. Since you know how much money is coming in you can budget accordingly, but when you own your own business, this changes quickly.

I was very blessed to get married soon after I opened my practice, so we had at least one steady income in our home. The existing debts and bills I had prior to saying, "I do," along with whatever bills Sedrick came to the marriage with, still had to be paid, and not having a consistent salary made this phase difficult.

I think not paying yourself has the potential to make you very bitter toward the people in your office who are getting paid. It's very important to value the work you do and your team's, regardless of the money you are or are not making. I remember there were times when my team would get paid and I could not pay myself, sometimes for weeks at a time. I recall several times when I would ask a team member to do something in the office and sensed an attitude or slothful response, and I would get so frustrated. I was thinking, *You're getting paid, and I'm not. The least you could do is what I ask, without an attitude.*

This is one of the unknown truths about owning a practice that few people see. So many people look at business owners as successful and wealthy. I clearly recall several patients and colleagues saying they thought I'd make a lot of money by owning my own practice. As a matter of fact, the common quote was, "Do you know how much money you're making for this dentist you work for? You could be making that for yourself."

The truth is, yes, once all of the practice debt is demolished, and the practice is profitable, those assumptions are true. However, many people are unaware of the meantime salary (or lack thereof) when they motivate you to step out on your own. Yes, there is a strong sense of achievement when owning your own practice because of the freedom, but the bottom line is you still need money. Before you open your own practice, start saving significant amounts of money. Put enough aside so that you'll have money to live off of before you start paying yourself. You should consider your personal budget in order to determine how much that amount should be. And once you are on salary, you may not be making as much as when working for someone else, so be prepared. This instability of your income should be temporary, even though in the beginning it can feel like an eternity. As my CPA recommended, about six months to a year into the practice, you should consider putting yourself on payroll. You deserve to get paid. It's important financially and also mentally. There is value behind the work you do everyday, and value needs to come back to you.

Another excellent suggestion is to secure a line of credit with a local bank or credit union. They typically work with small businesses much better than the big banks. Also consider obtaining a credit card that issues points toward travel, and use that card to pay your lab and supply bills. This will allow you to gain huge discounts on travel when you need it for business, and it also will give you a longer window of time to pay off the bills on the card if needed. This will keep you in good standing with your dental supply company and lab. Be sure to request these items when you first apply for the loan for the practice, because once you start the business, it can be extremely difficult to obtain new lines of credit. Having a large business loan already may cause lenders to be hesitant to approve you for more. And please remember, you are an important bill, so make yourself a priority.

CHAPTER 7

Giving

> One person gives freely, yet gains even more;
> another withholds unduly, but comes to poverty.
> (Proverbs 11:24)

Giving is something that I've always enjoyed doing. Whatever I give, be it my time, money, or other resources, giving has always been a part of life for me. As a Christian, I strongly believe in sowing and reaping, though millions of non-Christians also believe in the same principle of giving to others. Even wise financial advisors teach sowing and reaping, even if they are unaware that it is a biblical principle. Farmers sow and reap and they understand this reality intimately: if nothing is sown, nothing can be reaped. I honestly believe that everyone, no matter how large your practice is, should give something to someone or to some cause. "Each of you should give what you have decided in your heart to give, not reluctantly or under compulsion, for God loves a cheerful giver" (2 Corinthians 9:7 NIV). Tithing by definition is giving the first ten percent of your income. An offering is anything given above and beyond the tithe. Both of these principles are cited several times in the Old and New Testament of the Holy Bible (see Leviticus 27:30-32;

Numbers 18:26, 28; Deuteronomy 12:11; and Luke 11:42). There are over 450 scriptures in the Bible about the tithe and giving. Any topic mentioned that frequently in the Bible should be considered important. There are unlimited benefits to tithing and giving in general.

I know not everyone is a Christian; you may not follow biblical principles, but giving may be part of your religious beliefs. At some level in life, people typically decide whether or not they are going to sow (or give to someone or some cause bigger than them). This may be to a local youth group, a community organization, a civic cause, researching the cure for a disease, or a theater group. If you observe the most successful entrepreneurs in the world, they all have one thing in common: they all give to something.

Giving does not always need to be financial. You can give of your time, like in volunteering. Try not to think that giving your time is insignificant; time is the most valuable thing you can give anyone, since you can never get it back. Find a way to give something away. If done wisely, it will not destroy you or your practice. This principle can only bless you if done with the right motive. When focusing on sowing more, the reaping will come. Try not to consume yourself with what you will gain from giving. If you are giving just to receive something in return, the motive is wrong; this defeats the spirit of generosity. Keep your heart in check. Can you recall a time when someone unexpectedly gave you something, not for your birthday or a holiday? How did that make you feel? Have you ever given to someone unexpectedly? How did they react?

There have been times in my own life that I have done something for someone, and several weeks or months later, another unrelated person gave to me in a similar fashion. This is what some refer to as "harvest time," which can only come after sowing. Think in terms of gardening. Gardeners expect a harvest of the seeds they have sown. If they plant tomato seeds, they do not wait at harvest time for roses to bloom. In the same light, be aware of sowing and giving with the expectation of an instant harvest. It takes time, but be assured the harvest is coming. Even chia pets take a few weeks to fully bloom.

The Bible says, "Give, and it will be given to you. A good measure, pressed down, shaken together and running over, will be poured into your lap. For with the measure you use, it will be measured to you" (Luke 6:38 NIV). I have given money to various charitable organizations and may not have harvested money back from them directly, but I did receive unexpected opportunities from other sources; some sources brought cash into my hand, and others brought a return far greater than money.

The harvest is always greater than the seed sown. Participating in community outreach is a wonderful way to give of your resources and your talents as a dentist. In my practice, I often donated toothbrushes, toothpaste, or even free exams or treatment at community health fairs. Yes, participating in these events cost my practice money, but they were also rewarding for the entire team and a significant benefit to our community and the public we served.

Giving gifts to patients for milestones in their lives is another great way to give. This can be a twofold blessing to the practice. One, it shows the patients that you care. Two, it is a great marketing tool. Find a way to keep track of a patient's birthday, wedding anniversary, birth of children, major job promotions, their children's graduations, and even (sadly) the death of family members. Sending patients a small gift to acknowledge these milestones lets them know they are more than just another number in your practice; patients will know that you are aware of their lives and want to celebrate with them. These are patients you will potentially keep for life, along with those connected to them. It doesn't cost much to send someone a pair of theater or movie tickets. A gift card to a local restaurant or picking up some cupcakes is a great way to celebrate a patient's special day. How wonderful would it be to acknowledge the anniversary of them being cancer free? When their spouse returns from a military deployment, display the balloons in an area where other patients can see at the front desk, with a nice card of gratitude for their service to our country signed by each of your dental team.

We gave a nice gift basket full of kitchen gadgets to a patient who enjoys cooking. This was fun for us, and she was very grateful and faithful, along with her entire family. If your office budget allows, consider giving a gift certificate to a nearby smoothie or juice shop where patients can receive a free cold beverage after their dental appointment to enjoy while they recover from local anesthesia. Find a way to let your patients know that you value them as patients. I'd bet the farm they will be surprised and pleased.

Mentoring students is another way to give back. I let two local students shadow me in the office while I mentored them. One girl was in high school and spent a lot of her summer vacation in my office. The other was a college student from out of state who was interested in dentistry and spent the summer with a patient of mine. Both students were eager to learn about dentistry. The time they spent in the office was a learning experience for both of them, even though they both gained different experiences during their time shadowing me. The former high school student is currently a successful college student. The former undergraduate student recently got accepted to dental school. I am very excited about both of their futures. As they both become successful leaders, I hope they choose to share their time mentoring other young students someday.

Providing dental services to the underserved and patients with Medicaid was emotionally rewarding. I considered only providing care to low-income patients until I saw the reimbursement schedule with their insurance. Our low-income health care system is currently not designed to be profitable for dental practices. There are many private dental practices that serve this population of patients alone, but they tend to find themselves in potential compromising situations when the debt of the practice outweighs the income being made. Unfortunately, there are way too many of our dental colleagues who succumb to the temptation of insurance fraud in order to make up the balance between their debts and profits. Consider dedicating a portion of the weekly or monthly schedule to provide dental care to those who are underserved. Let your budget determine what that percentage of time will be in your office schedule. Serving others, knowing there may be little to no financial gain, provides a reward that money alone will never provide. Find some healthy way, some enjoyable way, and some rewarding way to give of your time, your talent, and your treasure. This will definitely be a long-term blessing to you and to your practice.

CHAPTER 8

Expansion

> Plan with the resources you have, not with the resources you hope to have.
>
> —Pastor Rick Godwin, Summit Christian Center, San Antonio, Texas

Expand your practice (I'm talking about physical expansion). I've read many articles concerning when and how to expand your office. Reading this material really sucked me in and hyped me up. I was so excited about having this extra room, I went out and accrued more debt in order to open a fourth operatory. My office space was three thousand square feet, and when we opened, we started out with three fully equipped operatories. However, close to our second year, we were so busy that I decided we needed a fourth operatory to manage the overflow. It was just like the articles said: if I opened another operatory, I would be compelled to keep it filled.

The unfortunate reality was that we did not actually need a fourth operatory; we just needed to manage our schedule more efficiently. We should have worked until people were falling out of the building before we invested in that fourth operatory. Revisiting one of the points I made earlier about paying yourself, the money I spent on that operatory could have been part of my much-needed take-home salary. Try not to get caught up in the hype of trends. Most of the people writing those trendy articles about what you need in your dental office have been in practice for twenty-plus years, with several years of profit (or they've never practiced at all).

The one good thing about my expansion was that I now had an overflow room, when needed. Once we managed our schedule better, we quickly realized that we didn't need that room as much as we thought we did. The room was very helpful when we found ourselves running behind or just wanted to serve patients who came in early for their appointment. When someone walked in with a dental emergency and the other operatories were full, this room was a perfect place to treat them. I was often able to use the operatory to adjust a filling or remove an orthodontic bracket. My assistant could polish a patient's teeth, take radiographs and make preliminary impressions, or apply fluoride while the hygienist or I completed treatment on another patient. We used this space, but at what cost? Having an extra operatory was obviously not a bad thing, but knowing the best time to invest in that extra room was the key. My office still had enough room for two additional operatories, and the ability to expand to a total of six.

Choosing a building that allows for growth and future expansion without having to relocate your office can be very beneficial. We should have considered starting out during the original practice build-out with a better foundational plan of how many we would need within the first five years. This would have allowed us to prepare in advance for outfitting those rooms. One way to reduce the cost of the addition is to have the plumbing, electrical wiring, lighting, etc., installed in advance, so when it is time to fully outfit another operatory, there will be little to no construction cost. You reduce the expense of re-hiring contractors, plumbers and electricians at the time of expansion, and would only have the expense of purchasing the dental chair and delivery system, which would be ready to plug and play.

It reminds me of when I was building my first home, and they asked if I wanted to upgrade the light fixtures. After further discussion with my mother, I found out that upgrading to the next level of lighting would have increased my monthly payment by less than a dollar per year over the life of the mortgage. The cost would have been significantly more had I decided to purchase newer fixtures after the home was completed. Slow down and take your time to consider which expansion choices are wiser for you to make on the front end versus the ones that should wait until the practice is profitable.

Expand the services you provide. As a new practice, we were fortunate to develop a relationship early on, with a government agency that referred several patients to us for their crowns and bridges to be fabricated. The exciting part for us was looking at the production at the end of a busy day of crown preparations. The not-so-exciting part was seeing most of that money go to the overall cost of crown and bridge lab fees, the required supplies to take impressions and make temporary crowns (sometimes multiple ones), and the cost of the chair time over two office visits. The production no longer looks as high when the expenses are factored in. At the time, the CAD/CAM systems that allow you to fabricate permanent crowns chairside while your patient waits were extremely expensive. If you have a practice that fabricates a lot of crowns and bridges, factor in the cost savings of owning one of those systems with respect to the money spent making crowns the traditional way. You may find that the CAD/CAM system is not as expensive anymore, and may actually be profitable for your practice. Patients are more likely to accept treatment if they can reduce their appointments and receive the work in the same day. We live in an instant world, where reducing someone's wait time is perceived as a plus to many.

Your service expansion does not have to be geared toward crown and bridge work, however, it should be something that can make your practice more functional and profitable, as well as meeting the needs of the patients you serve. Some offices offer an area dedicated to crafts or gaming centers for the young (and young at heart) to enjoy while waiting for their appointment. Those are not directly dental related, but keeping patients occupied while in the waiting room may help relieve their pre-appointment stress. Not to mention it also causes the sheer selfish motivation to return to the dental office to complete that craft project or to get to the next level on that game they started the previous visit. Thinking out of the box works, right?

Expand with your teammates. This is a big one. How many hygienists do you really need? How many assistants do you really need? How many people at the front desk do you really need? These are excellent questions that need to be answered before you open your practice and way before you start to hire your dental team. From the management perspective only, my idea of a perfect office would consist of one hygienist, one person at the front desk, and one dental assistant. I am truly laughing out loud right now because truth be told, I probably needed an army of people to get me through one of my busy days smoothly. This is sad but true, so I am laughing at that too.

Honestly, it depends on the type of practice you have and the type of procedures you're going to undertake. My office actually had two people at the front desk, two part-time hygienists (only one worked at a time), one full-time dental assistant, and one part-time dental assistant. The part-time assistant worked whenever the hygienist was present so that she could assist with the flow of two providers. I only had hygiene two days a week which was enough for the flow of patients we had at the time. I definitely needed two people at the front desk. I believe this is the very least needed to manage the front desk for any dental practice.

One thing I suggest is to have enough people in your office to answer the phones. That was something I was sure to train everyone, even the other dental team members, to do. Answering the phone and scheduling patients was very important, because if the ladies at the front desk were busy, anyone in the office could answer the phone and schedule a patient correctly. We used the "two-ring" rule, which means, the phone never rings more than twice without being answered. That was very important to me and should be to any great business. So many people lose business because they do not answer the phone in a timely manner. We also made sure to keep callers on hold for no more than two minutes. Patients will disconnect and may never call back, because they feel you do not value them or their time. Ask the caller if they mind holding for no more than two minutes, and wait for their response before placing them on hold. The caller may not be able to hold, and that's when you can have another team member step in and take over that call. Also, if you have placed a caller on hold, be sure to keep your word and return to their call before the two minutes is up.

Having a great dental assistant is very important; an assistant who not only knows their job well, but also knows you and has the best intentions for your patients and the practice. I started out with one full-time dental assistant, and over time realized I was wearing her out. She could only do so much by herself. One of the two front desk team members was also a trained dental assistant. She was able to step in and help turn over rooms, sterilize instruments, restock things, and come to the back and actually assist chairside when needed. The other bonus to the dental assistant's flexibility came into play with scheduling and discussing dental procedures with patients. She was very familiar with the time it took for me to do certain procedures and what those procedures entailed, so it was a bonus having her at the front desk to answer questions for patients and ensuring our schedule was practical. What a difference cross-training your dental team can make in your office.

I laugh at this statement, only because my office manager was completely grossed out over the sight of anything in someone else's mouth. This was sometimes a problem, especially when I needed her for something while I was in the operatory. She would literally stand outside the door and peek her head in just to ensure she didn't see anything she considered gross. She was great at the front desk, but made it very clear that she wanted nothing to do with what we were engaged in past that front desk.

The part-time dental assistant, who was employed specifically for when the hygienist was working, was a huge asset as well. Her duties included turning over rooms, sterilizing instruments, and assisting the hygienist with prophys and setting up new patients and taking x-rays for me and the hygienist. The two dental assistants swapped back-and-forth between me and the hygienist and any other office duties as needed. Wherever they were needed, they were faithfully there. It was a true tag team, and I really enjoyed working with them in that way.

No one particular assistant was assigned to me on the days I had the two of them. That made such a huge difference in the flow of the office and the flow of patients. One of my dental assistants spoke Spanish fluently. This was a huge help on days when we had patients who spoke no English. As a matter of fact, we encouraged those patients to schedule their appointments on the days she was in the office.

Ensuring that your staff is diverse in abilities helps

tremendously when it comes down to the comradery in the office. No one steps on anyone else's toes. Everyone works together as a team, and it truly becomes a family. There are times when you have to expand and hire new team members, and timing with this is just as important. Be sure to consult someone in a human resources firm or read a good book on how successful companies hire and fire team members, all for the best benefit and growth of the practice. Expansion of your practice, whether considering the space, the procedures offered, or the team is well worth the time it takes doing it the right way at the right time.

CHAPTER 9

To Broker or Not to Broker? That Is the Question

When the time comes to sell your practice, should you use a dental practice sales broker to help you sell it or not? The only reason I can come up with for *not* using a broker to sell your practice would be their commission percentage. Just like selling your home, you'll pay a percentage of the sale price to the broker. But, why *should* you use one? Because you don't know how to do their job, and the right brokerage firm does exceptional work. Think of it this way: we can do a MODBL amalgam on tooth #18 with our eyes closed, right? Can a sales broker? No way! For those non-dentists reading this, MODBL is the acronym for surfaces of a tooth and amalgam is the type of restoration material used to fill a cavity. So, when it comes to purchasing or selling a practice, in my opinion, having a broker is the only way to go.

Keep in mind that the most important step is locating a broker and firm that you connect with. If you only consider the number of sales or purchases they make, you'll miss the point of hiring a great broker. The broker represents you throughout the selling or purchasing process. They speak on your behalf. If you don't see eye to eye, their stats will mean nothing. Again, it is like a Realtor in the search for your home. The wrong match will keep you frustrated and, in the end, envious of your neighbor who had a Realtor who understood their desires. The broker I hired when selling my practice went beyond the call of duty for me; she did an excellent job. It was a very difficult sell for several reasons, mainly because it was classified as a short sale due to the limited time we were working with. We had several challenges with the buyer while facing the standard obstacles of selling a practice. Through it all, my broker maintained her integrity and business sense. She also helped to keep me sane throughout the lengthy process. The broker not only represented me with the seller, but with any other parties involved in the selling process.

You should be brutally honest with your broker from the start of any transition. They do represent you, but if you're not transparent with them, it will make their job very difficult. My situation was unique in that I needed to sell my practice because Sedrick, an active-duty Soldier in the US Army, was given orders to relocate our family to a new duty station almost fourteen hundred miles away. When I met with my broker, I explained that we needed to sell the practice as swiftly as possible so that I could relocate with my husband. Selling the practice versus managing it remotely ended up being agreat decision for us, because the distance between the practice and our new home was too far away to successfully continue to manage it. Choosing to hire a dental broker made this stressful and lengthy transition a success. You'll be glad you took the time to select the right dental broker for the purchase or sale of your practice.

CHAPTER 10

What Now?

Make failure your teacher, not your undertaker.

-Zig Ziglar

Many people ask, "Will you reopen your practice?" That's a question I still don't have an answer to. At times I do miss my dental team and the freedom of ownership, although right now being a sole practitioner isn't the answer for me due to the many relocations we have had across the U.S. with the military. I enjoy seeing the world and experiencing new people and places. Owning my own dental practice would keep me stationary and unable to experience life with my husband. For so many military spouses, this is a stressful decision to make, whether to continue in their successfully developed career versus embarking on the relocations every three to four years. I have been excited by the cultural diversity we have experienced across this country. I have no regrets making the decision I made to travel with Sedrick. Life is too precious to sit still. I want to see the world, literally. I know this is possible as a business owner, however I also know the practice would have to be run by someone else in order for it to succeed. I don't want my wings clipped, because I like soaring above the clouds like an eagle.

Owning my own practice was a valuable experience, and I wouldn't trade it for anything. So many valuable lessons emerged in the midst of it all. You cannot put a price on experience. I wish all of my colleagues the absolute best when embarking on the journey as a dental practice owner. There is a sense of pride and accomplishment that comes with establishing your own practice. This is to be commended. Somehow, in spite of the adversities I endured during my time as a sole practitioner and small business owner, I grew more than ever as a dentist, as a leader, as a wife, and more than anything, as a child of God. Since selling my dental practice, I've had several opportunities in the field of dentistry that have opened my perspective to a variety of career possibilities. I was offered the chance to work as an independent contractor, a locum dentist. The company I worked for covered all my travel expenses and the cost of licensures in various states. I filled in for dentists at their practice when they were out of the office for a variety of reasons. Some needed coverage when on vacation or medical leave, and one corporate practice needed a dentist while they sought a full-time permanent dentist.

I was able to travel to various states, mainly Pennsylvania and Michigan, along with my home base at the time, Texas. This was an excellent experience and allowed me to see different dental offices from an outsider's view. Because I was only at these locations for a few weeks at a time and had zero investment in these practices, I could observe the way offices were run and see what the owners of the practices may not have been privy to.

These various practices, in many cases, confirmed that the topics covered in this book are important to consider. Some of the practices I filled in at were well-oiled machines, while others struggled to an embarrassing degree. After the second relocation with my husband I decided that spending several weeks away from home and living out of a suitcase was not ideal for our family. I decided to apply for a dentist position with a government agency and was pleased when offered a public health position at a correctional facility. Talk about a different world from my fifteen-plus years in the dental field.

Even though this position is extremely different, it is very rewarding. I can help those who are unable to help themselves and earn the benefits of working for the government: forty-hour work week, no weekends, paid holidays, earned vacation days, and a retirement plan matched by the government. Yes, the variety of dental procedures that are typically offered in a private practice is not available, although if doing dentistry without the added stress of overseeing a dental team or being concerned with insurance companies and their rules appeals to you, consider dentistry in a public health setting.

This has been a great way to provide dentistry to a population of people who typically need help reprioritizing their lives in a healthy way, so that they do not return to prison in the future. I am currently the Chief of Dentistry overseeing the clinical aspects of twelve prisons across the state. The various dental experiences I've had throughout my career are a significant asset to this leadership position.

No matter how or where you choose to live out your dental career, be sure to enjoy it and make the very best of each and every day. Find a way to remind yourself why you chose dentistry in the first place. We've been given the gift of becoming a health care provider, and there is no mistake in saying this is a gift from God. Do your part in helping your community, nation, and world in whatever way you are led to help. Work diligently, rest peacefully, and help those following in your footsteps, knowing that when it's all said and done, you did your part in making this world a better place one healthy smile at a time.

References

Dental Association, A. (n.d.). Something to Smile About: Careers in the Dental Profession. Retrieved from www.nidcr.nih.gov

Ziglar, Z. (2004). Top Performance. Revell. Retrieved from https://www.ziglar.com/product/top-performance/

About the Author

 Dr. Joy N. McDaniel was born and raised in North Carolina. She graduated from Florida A&M University in Tallahassee, Florida, where she earned a bachelor's degree in psychology. She completed the country's first dental post-baccalaureate program at the University of California, San Francisco's School of Dentistry and completed her Doctor of Dental Medicine degree, in 2004, at Temple University School of Dentistry in Philadelphia, Pennsylvania. In 2009 Dr. McDaniel earned her Fellowship in the International Congress of Oral Implantologists. After opening her first dental practice, Oasis Dental, she met and married an active duty soldier. As a dedicated military spouse willing to relocate across the country when duty calls, Dr. McDaniel has had the opportunity to work in a variety of dental settings throughout the United States. This experience has given her valuable behind-the-scenes insight she is willing to share about owning and operating a dental practice.

Joy N. McDaniel, DMD, is an energetic, caring speaker who is available to present for your next dental-related event. Through Dr. McDaniel's wisdom and personal experience, she is able to teach on valuable topics such as these and more:

- The top five tips commonly missed before opening your own dental practice

- Creating an oasis environment for clients

- The do's and don'ts of selecting your dental team

- Surrounding yourself with competent experts

- Minorities in dentistry

- Unique dental career opportunities

- Other customized topics, based on your audience and needs

To book Dr. Joy McDaniel to speak or present for your next dental industry event, conference, graduation or training, contact her today at joynmcdaniel@yahoo.com.

You can also stay up-to-date on Dr. McDaniel's speaking engagements, classes and private coaching opportunities by also following her Facebook fan page at www.facebook/DrJoyMcDaniel.

CPSIA information can be obtained
at www.ICGtesting.com
Printed in the USA
BVHW031139270121
598893BV00006B/55